EPISTLES ON ARIANISM AND THE DEPOSITION OF ARIUS

St. Alexander of Alexandria

Dalcassian
Publishing
Company

PHILADELPHIA, PA

Translated by James B.H. Hawkins. From Ante-Nicene Fathers, Vol. 6. Edited by Alexander Roberts, James Donaldson, and A. Cleveland Coxe. (Buffalo, NY: Christian Literature Publishing Co., 1886.)

Library of Congress Cataloging-in-Publication Data

1. To Alexander, Bishop of the City of Constantinople

To the most reverend and like-minded brother, Alexander, Alexander sends greeting in the Lord:

1. The ambitious and avaricious will of wicked men is always wont to lay snares against those churches which seem greater, by various pretexts attacking the ecclesiastical piety of such. For incited by the devil who works in them, to the lust of that which is set before them, and throwing away all religious scruples, they trample under foot the fear of the judgment of God. Concerning which things, I who suffer, have thought it necessary to show to your piety, in order that you may be aware of such men, lest any of them presume to set foot in your dioceses, whether by themselves or by others; for these sorcerers know how to use hypocrisy to carry out their fraud; and to employ letters composed and dressed out with lies, which are able to deceive a man who is intent upon a simple and sincere faith. Arius, therefore, and Achilles, having lately entered into a conspiracy, emulating the ambition of Colluthus, have turned out far worse than he. For Colluthus, indeed, who reprehends these very men, found some pretext for his evil purpose; but these, beholding his battering of Christ, endured no longer to be subject to the Church; but building for themselves dens of thieves, they hold their assemblies in them unceasingly, night and day directing their calumnies against Christ and against us. For since they call in question all pious and apostolic doctrine, after the manner of the Jews, they have constructed a workshop for contending against Christ, denying the Godhead of our Saviour, and preaching that He is only the equal of all others. And having collected all the passages which speak of His plan of salvation and His humiliation for our sakes, they endeavour from these to collect the preaching of their impiety, ignoring altogether the passages in which His eternal Godhead and unutterable glory with the Father is set forth. Since, therefore, they back up the impious opinion concerning Christ, which is held by the Jews and Greeks, in every possible way they strive to gain their approval; busying themselves about all those things which they are wont to deride in us, and daily stirring up against us seditions and persecutions. And now, indeed, they drag us before the tribunals of the judges, by intercourse with silly and disorderly women, whom they have led into error; at another time they cast opprobrium and infamy upon the Christian religion, their young maidens disgracefully wandering about every village and street. Nay, even Christ's indivisible tunic, which His executioners were unwilling to divide, these wretches have dared to rend.

2. And we, indeed, though we discovered rather late, on account of their concealment, their manner of life, and their unholy attempts, by the common suffrage of all have cast them forth from the congregation of the Church

which adores the Godhead of Christ. But they, running here and there against us, have begun to betake themselves to our colleagues who are of the same mind with us; in appearance, indeed, pretending to seek for peace and concord, but in reality seeking to draw over some of them by fair words to their own diseases, asking long wordy letters from them, in order that reading these to the men whom they have deceived, they may make them impenitent in the errors into which they have fallen, and obdurate in impiety, as if they had bishops thinking the same thing and siding with them. Moreover, the things which among us they have wrongly taught and done, and on account of which they have been expelled by us, they do not at all confess to them, but they either pass them over in silence, or throwing a veil over them, by feigned words and writings they deceive them. Concealing, therefore, their pestilent doctrine by their specious and flattering discourse, they circumvent the more simple-minded and such as are open to fraud, nor do they spare in the meanwhile to traduce our piety to all. Hence it comes to pass that some, subscribing their letters, receive them into the Church, although in my opinion the greatest guilt lies upon those ministers who venture to do this; because not only does the apostolic rule not allow of it, but the working of the devil in these men against Christ is by this means more strongly kindled. Wherefore without delay, brethren beloved, I have stirred myself up to show you the faithlessness of these men who say that there was a time when the Son of God was not; and that He who was not before, came into existence afterwards, becoming such, when at length He was made, even as every man is wont to be born. For, they say, God made all things from things which are not, comprehending even the Son of God in the creation of all things rational and irrational. To which things they add as a consequence, that He is of mutable nature, and capable both of virtue and vice.And this hypothesis being once assumed, that He is from things which are not, they overturn the sacred writings concerning His eternity, which signify the immutability and the Godhead of Wisdom and the Word, which are Christ.

3. We, therefore, say these wicked men, can also be the sons of God even as He. For it is written, I have nourished and brought up children. Isaiah 1:2 But when what follows was objected to them, and they have rebelled against me, which indeed is not applicable to the nature of the Saviour, who is of an immutable nature; they, throwing off all religious reverence, say that God, since He foreknew and had foreseen that His Son would not rebel against Him, chose Him from all. For He did not choose Him as having by nature anything specially beyond His other sons, for no one is by nature a son of God, as they say; neither as having any peculiar property of His own; but God chose Him who was of a mutable nature, on account of the carefulness of His manners and His practice, which in no way turned to that which is evil; so that, if Paul and Peter had striven for this, there would have been no

difference between their sonship and His. And to confirm this insane doctrine, playing with Holy Scripture, they bring forward what is said in the Psalms respecting Christ: You love righteousness, and hate wickedness: therefore God, Your God, has anointed You with the oil of gladness above Your fellows,

4. But that the Son of God was not made from things which are not, and that there was no time when He was not, the evangelist John sufficiently shows, when he thus writes concerning Him: The only-begotten Son, who is in the bosom of the Father. John 1:18 For since that divine teacher intended to show that the Father and the Son are two things inseparable the one from the other, he spoke of Him as being in the bosom of the Father. Now that also the Word of God is not comprehended in the number of things that were created from things which are not, the same John says, All things were made by Him. For he set forth His proper personality, saying, In the beginning was the Word, and the Word was with God, and the Word was God. All things were made by Him; and with out Him was not anything made that was made. John 1:1-3 For if all things were made by Him, how comes it that He who gave to the things which are made their existence, at one time Himself was not. For the Word which makes is not to be defined as being of the same nature with the things which are made; since He indeed was in the beginning, and all things were made by Him, and fashioned from things which are not.Moreover, that which is seems to be contrary to and far removed from those things which are made from things which are not. For that indeed shows that there is no interval between the Father and the Son, since not even in thought can the mind imagine any distance between them.But that the world was created from things which are not, indicates a more recent and a later origin of substance, since the universe receives an essence of this sort from the Father by the Son. When, therefore, the most pious John contemplated the essence of the divine Word at a very great distance, and as placed beyond all conception of those things that are begotten, he thought it not meet to speak of His generation and creation; not daring to designate the Creator in the same terms as the things that are made. Not that the Word is unbegotten, for the Father alone is unbegotten, but because the inexplicable subsistence of the only-begotten Son transcends the acute comprehension of the evangelists, and perhaps also of angels.

5. Wherefore I do not think that he is to be reckoned among the pious who presumes to inquire into anything beyond these things, not listening to this saying: Seek not out the things that are too hard for you, neither search the things that are above your strength. For if the knowledge of many other things that are incomparably inferior to this, are hidden from human comprehension, such as in the apostle Paul, Eye has not seen, nor ear heard, neither have entered into the heart of man, the things which God has

prepared for them that love Him. 1 Corinthians 2:9 As also God said to Abraham, that he could not number the stars; Genesis 15:5 and that passage, Who can number the sand of the sea, and the drops of rain Sirach 1:2 How shall any one be able to investigate too curiously the subsistence of the divine Word, unless he be smitten with frenzy? Concerning which the Spirit of prophecy says, Who shall declare his generation? Isaiah 53:8 And our Saviour Himself, who blesses the pillars of all things in the world, sought to unburden them of the knowledge of these things, saying that to comprehend this was quite beyond their nature, and that to the Father alone belonged the knowledge of this most divine mystery. For no man, says He, knows the Son, but the Father: neither knows any man the Father, save the Son. Matthew 11:27 Of this thing also I think that the Father spoke, in the words, My secret is to Me and Mine.

6. Now that it is an insane thing to think that the Son was made from things which are not, and was in being in time, the expression, from things which are not, itself shows, although these stupid men understand not the insanity of their own words. For the expression, was not, ought either to be reckoned in time, or in some place of an age. But if it be true that all things were made by Him, it is established that both every age and time and all space, and that when in which the was not is found, was made by Him. And is it not absurd that He who fashioned the times and the ages and the seasons, in which that was not is mixed up, to say of Him, that He at some time was not? For it is devoid of sense, and a mark of great ignorance, to affirm that He who is the cause of everything is posterior to the origin of that thing. For according to them, the space of time in which they say that the Son had not yet been made by the Father, preceded the wisdom of God that fashioned all things, and the Scripture speaks falsely according to them, which calls Him the First-born of every creature. Conformable to which, that which the majestically-speaking Paul says of Him: Whom He has appointed heir of all things. By whom also He made the worlds. But by Him also were all things created that are in heaven, and that are in earth, visible and invisible, whether they be thrones or dominions, or principalities, or powers; all things were created by Him, and for Him; and He is before all things. Colossians 1:16-17

7. Wherefore, since it appears that this hypothesis of a creation from things which are not is most impious, it is necessary to say that the Father is always the Father. But He is the Father, since the Son is always with Him, on account of whom He is called the Father. Wherefore, since the Son is always with Him, the Father is always perfect, being destitute of nothing as regards good; who, not in time, nor after an interval, nor from things which are not, has begotten His only-begotten Son. How, then, is it not impious to say, that the wisdom of God once was not which speaks thus concerning itself: I was with Him forming all things; I was His delight; or that the power of God once

did not exist; or that His Word was at any time mutilated; or that other things were ever wanting from which the Son is known and the Father expressed? For he who denies that the brightness of the glory existed, takes away also the primitive light of which it is the brightness. And if the image of God was not always, it is clear also that He was not always, of which it is the image. Moreover, in saying that the character of the subsistence of God was not, He also is done away with who is perfectly expressed by it. Hence one may see that the Sonship of our Saviour has nothing at all in common with the sonship of the rest. For just as it has been shown that His inexplicable subsistence excels by an incomparable excellence all other things to which He has given existence, so also His Sonship, which is according to the nature of the Godhead of the Father, transcends. by an ineffable excellence. the sonship of those who have been adopted by Him. For He, indeed, is of an immutable nature, every way perfect, and wanting in nothing; but these since they are either way subject to change, stand in need of help from Him. For what progress can the wisdom of God make? What increase can the truth itself and God the Word receive? In what respect can the life and the true light be made better? And if this be so, how much more unnatural is it that wisdom should ever be capable of folly; that the power of God should be con-joined with infirmity; that reason should be obscured by unreason; or that darkness should be mixed up with the true light? And the apostle says, on this place, What communion has light with darkness? And what concord has Christ with Belial? 2 Corinthians 6:14-15 And Solomon says, that it is not possible that it should come to pass that a man should comprehend with his understanding the way of a serpent upon a rock, which is Christ, according to the opinion of Paul. But men and angels, who are His creatures, have received His blessing that they might make progress, exercising themselves in virtues and in the commandments of the law, so as not to sin. Wherefore our Lord, since He is by nature the Son of the Father, is by all adored. But these, laying aside the spirit of bondage, when by brave deeds and by progress they have received the spirit of adoption, being blessed by Him who is the Son by nature, are made sons by adoption.

8. And His proper and peculiar, natural and excellent Sonship, St. Paul has declared, who thus speaks of God: Who spared not His own Son, but for us, who were not His natural sons, delivered Him up. Romans 8:32 For to distinguish Him from those who are not properly sons, He said that He was His own Son. And in the Gospel we read: This is My beloved Son, in whom I am well pleased. Matthew 3:17 Moreover, in the Psalms the Saviour says: The Lord has said to Me, You are my Son. Where, showing that He is the true and genuine Son, He signifies that there are no other genuine sons besides Himself. And what, too, is the meaning of this: From the womb before the morning I begot you? Does He not plainly indicate the natural sonship of

paternal bringing forth, which he obtained not by the careful framing of His manners, not by the exercise of and increase in virtue, but by property of nature? Wherefore, the only-begotten Son of the Father, indeed, possesses an indefectible Sonship; but the adoption of rational sons belongs not to them by nature, but is prepared for them by the probity of their life, and by the free gift of God. And it is mutable as the Scripture recognises: For when the sons of God saw the daughters of men, they took them wives, Genesis 6:2 etc. And in another place: I have nourished and brought up children, but they have rebelled against Me, Isaiah 1:2 as we find God speaking by the prophet Isaiah.

9. And though I could say much more, brethren beloved, I purposely omit to do so, as deeming it to be burdensome at great length to call these things to the remembrance of teachers who are of the same mind with myself. For you yourselves are taught of God, nor are you ignorant that this doctrine, which has lately raised its head against the piety of the Church, is that of Ebion and Artemas; nor is it anything else but an imitation of Paul of Samosata, bishop of Antioch, who, by the judgment and counsel of all the bishops, and in every place, was separated from the Church. To whom Lucian succeeding, remained for many years separate from the communion of three bishops. And now lately having drained the dregs of their impiety, there have arisen among us those who teach this doctrine of a creation from things which are not, their hidden sprouts, Arius and Achilles, and the gathering of those who join in their wickedness. And three bishops in Syria, having been, in some manner, consecrated on account of their agreement with them, incite them to worse things. But let the judgment concerning these be reserved for your trial. For they, retaining in their memory the words which came to be used with respect to His saving Passion, and abasement, and examination, and what they call His poverty, and in short of all those things to which the Saviour submitted for our sakes, bring them forward to refute His supreme and eternal Godhead. But of those words which signify His natural glory and nobility, and abiding with the Father, they have become unmindful. Such as this: I and My Father are one, John 10:30 which indeed the Lord says, not as proclaiming Himself to be the Father, nor to demonstrate that two persons are one; but that the Son of the Father most exactly preserves the expressed likeness of the Father, inasmuch as He has by nature impressed upon Him His similitude in every respect, and is the image of the Father in no way discrepant, and the expressed figure of the primitive exemplar. Whence, also, to Philip, who then was desirous to see Him, the Lord shows this abundantly. For when he said, Show us the Father, John 14:8-9 He answered: He that has seen Me, has seen the Father, since the Father was Himself seen through the spotless and living mirror of the divine image.Similar to which is what the saints say in the Psalms: In Your light shall we see light. Wherefore he that

honours the Son, honours the Father also; and with reason, for every impious word which they dare to speak against the Son, has reference to the Father.

10. But after these things, brethren beloved, what is there wonderful in that which I am about to write, if I shall set forth the false calumnies against me and our most pious laity? For those who have set themselves in array against the Godhead of Christ, do not scruple to utter their ungrateful ravings against us. Who will not either that any of the ancients should be compared with them, or suffer that any of those whom, from our earliest years, we have used as instructors should be placed on a level with them. Nay, and they do not think that any of all those who are now our colleagues, has attained even to a moderate amount of wisdom; boasting themselves to be the only men who are wise and divested of worldly possessions, the sole discoverers of dogmas, and that to them alone are those things revealed which have never before come into the mind of any other under the sun. Oh, the impious arrogance! Oh, the immeasurable madness! Oh, the vainglory befitting those that are crazed! Oh, the pride of Satan which has taken root in their unholy souls. The religious perspicuity of the ancient Scriptures caused them no shame, nor did the consentient doctrine of our colleagues concerning Christ keep in check their audacity against Him. Their impiety not even the demons will bear, who are ever on the watch for a blasphemous word uttered against the Son.

11. And let these things be now urged according to our power against those who, with respect to matter which they know nothing of, have, as it were, rolled in the dust against Christ, and have taken in hand to calumniate our piety towards Him. For those inventors of stupid fables say, that we who turn away with aversion from the impious and unscriptural blasphemy against Christ, of those who speak of His coming from the things which are not assert, that there are two unbegottens. For they ignorantly affirm that one of two things must necessarily be said, either that He is from things which are not, or that there are two unbegottens; nor do those ignorant men know how great is the difference between the unbegotten Father, and the things which were by Him created from things which are not, as well the rational as the irrational. Between which two, as holding the middle place, the only begotten nature of God, the Word by which the Father formed all things out of nothing, was begotten of the true Father Himself. As in a certain place the Lord Himself testified, saying, Every one that loves Him that begot, loves Him also that is begotten of Him. John 5:1

12. Concerning whom we thus believe, even as the Apostolic Church believes. In one Father unbegotten, who has from no one the cause of His being, who is unchangeable and immutable, who is always the same, and admits of no increase or diminution; who gave to us the Law, the prophets, and the Gospels; who is Lord of the patriarchs and apostles, and all the saints. And in

one Lord Jesus Christ, the only-begotten Son of God; not begotten of things which are not, but of Him who is the Father; not in a corporeal manner, by excision or division as Sabellius and Valentinus thought, but in a certain inexplicable and unspeakable manner, according to the words of the prophet cited above: Who shall declare His generation? Isaiah 53:8 Since that His subsistence no nature which is begotten can investigate, even as the Father can be investigated by none; because that the nature of rational beings cannot receive the knowledge of His divine generation by the Father. But men who are moved by the Spirit of truth, have no need to learn these things from me, for in our ears are sounding the words before uttered by Christ on this very thing, No man knows the Father, save the Son; and no man knows who the Son is, save the Father. Matthew 11:27 That He is equally with the Father unchangeable and immutable, wanting in nothing, and the perfect Son, and like to the Father, we have learned; in this alone is He inferior to the Father, that He is not unbegotten. For He is the very exact image of the Father, and in nothing differing from Him. For it is clear that He is the image fully containing all things by which the greatest similitude is declared, as the Lord Himself has taught us, when He says, My Father is greater than I. John 14:28 And according to this we believe that the Son is of the Father, always existing. For He is the brightness of His glory, the express image of His *Father's* person. Hebrews 1:3 But let no one take that word *always* so as to raise suspicion that He is unbegotten, as they imagine who have their senses blinded. For neither are the words, He was, or always, or before all worlds, equivalent to unbegotten. But neither can the human mind employ any other word to signify unbegotten. And thus I think that you understand it, and I trust to your right purpose in all things, since these words do not at all signify unbegotten. For these words seem to denote simply a lengthening out of time, but the Godhead, and as it were the antiquity of the only-begotten, they cannot worthily signify; but they have been employed by holy men, while each, according to his capacity, seeks to express this mystery, asking indulgence from the hearers, and pleading a reasonable excuse, in saying, Thus far have we attained. But if there be any who are expecting from mortal lips some word which exceeds human capacity, saying that those things have been done away which are known in part, it is manifest that the words, He was, and always, and before all ages, come far short of what they hoped. And whatever word shall be employed is not equivalent to unbegotten. Therefore to the unbegotten Father, indeed, we ought to preserve His proper dignity, in confessing that no one is the cause of His being; but to the Son must be allotted His fitting honour, in assigning to Him, as we have said, a generation from the Father without beginning, and allotting adoration to Him, so as only piously and properly to use the words, He was, and always, and before all worlds, with respect to Him; by no means rejecting His Godhead, but ascribing to Him a similitude which exactly answers in every respect to the

Image and Exemplar of the Father. But we must say that to the Father alone belongs the property of being unbegotten, for the Saviour Himself said, My Father is greater than I. John 14:28 And besides the pious opinion concerning the Father and the Son, we confess to one Holy Spirit, as the divine Scriptures teach us; who has inaugurated both the holy men of the Old Testament, and the divine teachers of that which is called the New. And besides, also, one only Catholic and Apostolic Church, which can never be destroyed, though all the world should seek to make war with it; but it is victorious over every most impious revolt of the heretics who rise up against it. For her Goodman has confirmed our minds by saying, Be of good cheer, I have overcome the world. John 16:33 After this we know of the resurrection of the dead, the first-fruits of which was our Lord Jesus Christ, who in very deed, and not in appearance merely, carried a body, of Mary Mother of God, who in the end of the world came to the human race to put away sin, was crucified and died, and yet did He not thus perceive any detriment to His divinity, being raised from the dead, taken up into heaven, seated at the right hand of majesty.

13. These things in part have I written in this epistle, thinking it burdensome to write out each accurately, even as I said before, because they escape not your religious diligence. Thus do we teach, thus do we preach. These are the apostolic doctrines of the Church, for which also we die, esteeming those but little who would compel us to forswear them, even if they would force us by tortures, and not casting away our hope in them. To these Arius and Achilles opposing themselves, and those who with them are the enemies of the truth, have been expelled from the Church, as being aliens from our holy doctrine, according to the blessed Paul, who says, If any man preach any other gospel unto you than that you have received, let him be accursed; even though he feign himself an angel from heaven. Galatians 1:8-9 And also, If any man teach otherwise, and consent not to the wholesome words of our Lord Jesus Christ, and to the doctrine which is according to godliness; he is proud, knowing nothing, 1 Timothy 6:3-4 and so forth. These, therefore, who have been anathematized by the brotherhood, let no one of you receive, nor admit of those things which are either said or written by them. For these seducers do always lie, nor will they ever speak the truth. They go about the cities, attempting nothing else but that under the mark of friendship and the name of peace, by their hypocrisy and blandishments, they may give and receive letters, to deceive by means of these a few silly women, and laden with sins, who have been led captive by them, 2 Timothy 3:4 and so forth.

14. These men, therefore, who have dared such things against Christ; who have partly in public derided the Christian religion; partly seek to traduce and inform against its professors before the judgment-seats; who in a time of peace, as far as in them lies, have stirred up a persecution against us; who have enervated the ineffable mystery of Christ's generation; from these, I say,

beloved and like-minded brethren, turning away in aversion, give your suffrages with us against their mad daring; even as our colleagues have done, who being moved with indignation, have both written to us letters against these men, and have subscribed our letter. Which also I have sent unto you by my son Apion the deacon, being some of them from the whole of Egypt and the Thebaid, some from Libya and Pentapolis. There are others also from Syria, Lycia, Pamphylia, Asia, Cappadocia, and the other neighbouring provinces. After the example of which I trust also that I shall receive letters from you. For though I have prepared many helps towards curing those who have suffered injury, this is the special remedy that has been devised for healing the multitudes that have been deceived by them, that they may comply with the general consent of our colleagues, and thus hasten to return to repentance. Salute one another, together with the brethren who are with you. I pray that you may be strong in the Lord, beloved, and that I may profit by your love towards Christ.

2. Epistle Catholic.

To our beloved and most reverend fellow-ministers of the Catholic Church in every place, Alexander sends greeting in the Lord:

1. Since the body of the Catholic Church is one, and it is commanded in Holy Scripture that we should keep the bond of unanimity and peace, it follows that we should write and signify to one another the things which are done by each of us; that whether one member suffer or rejoice we may all either suffer or rejoice with one another. In our diocese, then, not so long ago, there have gone forth lawless men, and adversaries of Christ, teaching men to apostatize; which thing, with good right, one might suspect and call the precursor of Antichrist. I indeed wished to cover the matter up in silence, that so perhaps the evil might spend itself in the leaders of the heresy alone, and that it might not spread to other places and defile the ears of any of the more simple-minded. But since Eusebius, the present bishop of Nicomedia, imagining that with him rest all ecclesiastical matters, because, having left Berytus and cast his eyes upon the church of the Nicomedians, and no punishment has been inflicted upon him, he is set over these apostates, and has undertaken to write everywhere, commending them, if by any means he may draw aside some who are ignorant to this most disgraceful and Antichristian heresy; it became necessary for me, as knowing what is written in the law, no longer to remain silent, but to announce to you all, that you may know both those who have become apostates, and also the wretched words of their heresy; and if Eusebius write, not to give heed to him.

2. For he, desiring by their assistance to renew that ancient wickedness of his mind, with respect to which he has for a time been silent, pretends that he is

writing in their behalf, but he proves by his deed that he is exerting himself to do this on his own account. Now the apostates from the Church are these: Arius, Achilles, Aithales, Carpones, the other Arius, Sarmates, who were formerly priests; Euzoius, Lucius, Julius, Menas, Helladius, and Gains, formerly deacons; and with them Secundus and Theonas, who were once called bishops. And the words invented by them, and spoken contrary to the mind of Scripture, are as follows:—

God was not always the Father; but there was a time when God was not the Father. The Word of God was not always, but was made 'from things that are not;' for He who is God fashioned the non-existing from the non-existing; wherefore there was a time when He was not. For the Son is a thing created, and a thing made: nor is He like to the Father in substance; nor is He the true and natural Word of the Father; nor is He His true Wisdom; but He is one of the things fashioned and made. And He is called, by a misapplication of the terms, the Word and Wisdom, since He is Himself made by the proper Word of God, and by that wisdom which is in God, in which, as God made all other things, so also did He make Him. Wherefore, He is by His very nature changeable and mutable, equally with other rational beings. The Word, too, is alien and separate from the substance of God. The father also is ineffable to the Son; for neither does the Word perfectly and accurately know the Father, neither can He perfectly see Him. For neither does the Son indeed know His own substance as it is. Since He for our sakes was made, that by Him as by an instrument God might create us; nor would He have existed had not God wished to make us. Some one asked of them whether the Son of God could change even as the devil changed; and they feared not to answer that He can; for since He was made and created, He is of mutable nature.

3. Since those about Arius speak these things and shamelessly maintain them, we, coming together with the Bishops of Egypt and the Libyas, nearly a hundred in number, have anathematized them, together with their followers. But those about Eusebius have received them, earnestly endeavouring to mix up falsehood with truth, impiety with piety. But they will not prevail; for the truth prevails, and there is no communion between light and darkness, no concord between Christ and Belial.2 Corinthians 6:14 For who ever heard such things? Or who, now hearing them, is not astonished, and does not stop his ears that the pollution of these words should not touch them? Who that hears John saying, In the beginning was the Word, John 1:1 does not condemn those who say there was a time when He was not? Who that hears these words of the Gospel, the only-begotten Son; John 1:18 and, by Him were all things made, John 1:3 will not hate those who declare He is one of the things made? For how can He be one of the things made by Him? Or how shall He be the only-begotten who, as they say, is reckoned with all the rest, if indeed He is a thing made and created? And how can He be made of

things which are not, when the Father says, My heart belched forth a good Word; and, From the womb, before the morning have I begotten You? Or how is He unlike to the substance of the Father, who is the perfect image and brightness of the Father, and who says, He that has seen Me has seen the Father? John 14:9 And how, if the Son is the Word or Wisdom and Reason of God, was there a time when He was not? It is all one as if they said, that there was a time when God was without reason and wisdom. How, also, can He be changeable and mutable, who says indeed by Himself: I am in the Father, and the Father in Me, John 14:10 and, I and My Father are one; John 10:30 and by the prophet, I am the Lord, I change not? Malachi 3:6 For even though one saying may refer to the Father Himself, yet it would now be more aptly spoken of the Word, because when He became man, He changed not; but, as says the apostle, Jesus Christ, the same yesterday, today, and forever. Hebrews 13:8 Who has induced them to say, that for our sakes He was made; although Paul says, for whom are all things, and by whom are all things? Hebrews 11:10

4. Now concerning their blasphemous assertion who say that the Son does not perfectly know the Father, we need not wonder: for having once purposed in their mind to wage war against Christ, they impugn also these words of His, As the Father knows Me, even so know I the Father. John 10:15 Wherefore, if the Father only in part knows the Son, then it is evident that the Son does not perfectly know the Father. But if it be wicked thus to speak, and if the Father perfectly knows the Son, it is plain that, even as the Father knows His own Word, so also the Word knows His own Father, of whom He is the Word.

5. By saying these things, and by unfolding the divine Scriptures, we have often refuted them. But they, chameleon-like, changing their sentiments, endeavour to claim for themselves that saying: When the wicked comes, then comes contempt. Proverbs 18:3 Before them, indeed, many heresies existed, which, having dared more than was right, have fallen into madness. But these by all their words have attempted to do away with the Godhead of Christ, have made those seem righteous, since they have come nearer to Antichrist. Wherefore they have been excommunicated and anathematized by the Church. And indeed, although we grieve at the destruction of these men, especially that after having once learned the doctrine of the Church, they have now gone back; yet we do not wonder at it; for this very thing Hymenaeus and Philetus suffered,2 Timothy 2:17 and before them Judas, who, though he followed the Saviour, afterwards became a traitor and an apostate. Moreover, concerning these very men, warnings are not wanting to us, for the Lord foretold: Take heed that you be not deceived: for many shall come in My name, saying, I am Christ; and the tithe draws near: go not therefore after them. Luke 21:8 Paul, too, having learned these things from the Saviour,

wrote, In the latter times some shall depart from the faith, giving heed to seducing spirits, and doctrines of devils which turn away from the truth. 1 Timothy 4:1

6. Since, therefore, our Lord and Saviour Jesus Christ has thus Himself exhorted us, and by His apostle has signified such things to us; we, who have heard their impiety with our own ears, have consistently anathematized such men, as I have already said, and have declared them to be aliens from the Catholic Church and faith, and we have made known the thing, beloved and most honoured fellow-ministers, to your piety, that you should not receive any of them, should they venture rashly to come unto you, and that you should not trust Eusebius or any one else who writes concerning them. For it becomes us as Christians to turn with aversion from all who speak or think against Christ, as the adversaries of God and the destroyers of souls, and not even to wish them Godspeed, lest at any time we become partakers of their evil deeds, as the blessed John enjoins. Salute the brethren who are with you. Those who are with me salute you. Presbyters of Alexandria.

I, Colluthus, presbyter, give my suffrage to the things which are written, and also for the deposition of Arius, and those who are guilty of impiety with him.

Alexander, presbyter
Arpocration, presbyter
Dioscorus, presbyter
Agathus, presbyter
Nemesius, presbyter
Dionysius, presbyter
Longus, presbyter
Silvanus, presbyter
Eusebius, presbyter
Perous, presbyter
Apis, presbyter
Alexander, presbyter
Proterius, presbyter
Paulus, presbyter
Nilaras, presbyter
Cyrus, presbyter
Ammonius, deacon
Ambytianus, deacon
Gaius, deacon
Macarius, deacon
Pistus, deacon
Alexander, deacon
Dionysius, deacon

Athanasius, deacon
Agathon, deacon
Eumenes, deacon
Polybius, deacon
Apollonius, deacon
Olympius, deacon
Theonas, deacon
Aphthonius, deacon
Marcus, deacon
Athanasius, deacon.
Commodus, deacon
Macarius, deacon
Serapion, deacon
Nilus, deacon
Paulus, deacon
Romanus, deacon
Petrus, deacon

Presbyters of Mareotis.

I, Apollonius, presbyter, give my suffrage to the things which are written, and also for the deposition of Arius, and of those who are guilty of impiety with him.

Ingenius, presbyter
Dioscorus, presbyter
Sostras, presbyter
Ammonius, presbyter
Theon, presbyter
Tyrannus, presbyter
Boccon, presbyter
Copres, presbyter
Agathus, presbyter
Ammonas, presbyter
Achilles, presbyter
Orion, presbyter
Paulus, presbyter
Serenus, presbyter
Thalelaeus, presbyter
Didymus, presbyter
Dionysius, presbyter
Heracles, presbyter
Sarapion, deacon
Didymus, deacon

Ptollarion, deacon
Justus, deacon
Seras, deacon
Gaius, deacon
Didymus, deacon
Hierax, deacon
Demetrius, deacon
Marcus, deacon
Maurus, deacon
Theonas, deacon
Alexander, deacon
Sarmaton, deacon
Marcus, deacon
Carpon, deacon
Comon, deacon
Zoilus, deacon
Tryphon, deacon
Ammonius, deacon

3. Epistle.

Alexander, to the priests and deacons, Alexandria and Mareotis, being present to them present, brethren beloved in the Lord, sends greeting:

Although you have been forward to subscribe the letters that I sent to those about Arius, urging them to abjure their impiety, and to obey the wholesome and Catholic faith; and in this manner have shown your orthodox purpose, and your agreement in the doctrines of the Catholic Church; yet because I have also sent letters to all our fellow-ministers in every place with respect to the things which concern Arius and his companions; I have thought it necessary to call together you the clergy of the city, and to summon you also of Mareotis; especially since of your number Chares and Pistus, the priests; Sarapion, Parammon, Zosimus, and Irenaeus, the deacons, have gone over to the party of Arius, and have preferred to be deposed with them; that you may know what is now written, and that you should declare your consent in these matters, and give your suffrage for the deposition of those about Arius and Pistus. For it is fight that you should know what I have written, and that you should each one, as if he had written it himself retain it in his heart.

4. Epistle to Aeglon, Bishop of Cynopolis, Against the Arians.

From a letter of St. Alexander, bishop of Alexandria, to Aeglon, bishop of Cynopolis, against the Arians.

1. Natural will is the free faculty of every intelligent nature as having nothing involuntary which is in respect of its essence.

2. Natural operation is the innate motion of all substance. Natural operation is the substantial and notifying reason of every nature. Natural operation is the notifying virtue of every substance.

5. On the Soul and Body and the Passion of the Lord.

1. The Word which is ungrudgingly sent down from heaven, is fitted for the irrigation of our hearts, if we have been prepared for His power, not by speaking only, but by listening. For as the rain without the ground does not produce fruit, so neither does the Word fructify without hearing, nor hearing without the Word. Moreover, the Word then becomes fruitful when we pronounce it, and in the same way hearing, when we listen. Therefore since the Word draws forth its power, do you also ungrudgingly lend your ears, and when you come to hear, cleanse yourselves from all ill-will and unbelief. Two very bad things are ill-will and unbelief, both of which are contrary to righteousness; for ill-will is opposed to charity, and unbelief to faith; just in the same way as bitterness is opposed to sweetness, darkness to light, evil to good, death to life, falsehood to truth. Those, therefore, who abound in these vices that are repugnant to virtue, are in a manner dead; for the malignant and the unbelieving hate charity and faith, and they who do this are the enemies of God.

2. Since therefore you know, brethren beloved, that the malignant and the unbelieving are the enemies of righteousness, beware of these, embrace faith and charity, by which all the holy men who have existed from the beginning of the world to this day have attained unto salvation. And show forth the fruit of charity, not in words only, but also in deeds, that is, in all godly patience for God's sake. For, see! The Lord Himself has shown His charity towards us, not only in words but also in deeds, since He has given Himself up as the price of our salvation. Besides, we were not created, like the rest of the world, by word alone, but also by deed. For God made the world to exist by the power of a single word, but us He produced by the efficacy alike of His word and working. For it was not enough for God to say, Let us make man in our image, after our likeness, Genesis 1:26 but deed followed word; for, taking the dust from the ground, He formed man out of it, conformable to His image and similitude, and into him He breathed the breath of life, so that Adam became a living soul.

3. But when man afterwards by his fall had inclined to death, it was necessary that that form should be recreated anew to salvation by the same Artificer. For the form indeed lay rotting in the ground; but that inspiration which had

been as the breath of life, was detained separate from the body in a dark place, which is called Hades. There was, therefore, a division of the soul from the body; it was banished *ad inferos*, while the latter was resolved into dust; and there was a great interval of separation between them; for the body, by the dissolution of the flesh, becomes corrupt; the soul being loosened from it, its action ceases. For as when the king is thrown into chains, the city falls to ruin; or as when the general is taken captive, the army is scattered abroad; or as when the helmsman is shaken off, the vessel is submerged; so when the soul is bound in chains, its body goes to pieces; as the city without its king, so its members are dissolved; as is the case with an army when its general is lost, they are drowned in death, even as happens to a vessel when deprived of its helmsman. The soul, therefore, governed the man, as long as the body survived; even as the king governs the city, the general the army, the helmsman the ship. But it was powerless to rule it, from the time when it was immoveably tied to it, and became immersed in error; therefore it was that it declined from the straight path, and followed tempters, giving heed to fornication, idolatry, and shedding of blood; by which evil deeds it has destroyed the proper manhood. Nay, but itself also being carried at length to the lower regions, it was there detained by the wicked tempter. Else was it wont, as the king restores the ruined city, the general collects the dispersed army, the sailor repairs the broken ship, even so, I say, the soul used to minister supplies to the body before that the body was dissolved in the dust, being not as yet itself bound fast with fetters. But after that the soul became bound, not with material fetters but with sins, and thus was rendered impotent to act, then it left its body in the ground, and being cast down to the lower regions, it was made the footstool of death, and despicable to all.

4. Man went forth from paradise to a region which was the sink of unrighteousness, fornication, adultery, and cruel murder. And there he found his destruction; for all things conspired to his death, and worked the ruin of him who had hardly entered there. Meanwhile man wanted some consolation and assistance and rest. For when was it well with man? In his mother's womb? But when he was shut up there, he differed but little from the dead. When he was nourished with milk from the breast? Not even then, indeed, did he feel any joy. Was it rather while he was coming to maturity? But then, especially, danger's impended over him from his youthful lusts. Was it, lastly, when he grew old? Nay, but then does he begin to groan, being pressed down by the weight of old age, and the expectation of death. For what else is old age but the expectation of death? Verily all the inhabitants of earth do die, young men and old, little children and adults, for no age or bodily stature is exempt from death. Why, then, is man tormented by this exceeding grief? Doubtless the very aspect of death begets sadness; for we behold in a dead man the face changed, the figure dead, the body shrunk up with emaciation,

the mouth silent, the skin cold, the carcass prostrate on the ground, the eyes sunken, the limbs immoveable, the flesh wasted away, the veins congealed, the bones whitened, the joints dissolved, all parts of him reduced to dust, and the man no longer existing. What, then, is man? A flower, I say, that is but for a little time, which in his mother's womb is not apparent, in youth flourishes, but which in old age withers and departs in death.

5. But now, after all this bondage to death and corruption of the manhood, God has visited His creature, which He formed after His own image and similitude; and this He has done that it might not for ever be the sport of death. Therefore God sent down from heaven His incorporeal Son to take flesh upon Him in the Virgin's womb; and thus, equally as you, was He made man; to save lost man, and collect all His scattered members. For Christ, when He joined the manhood to His person, united that which death by the separation of the body had dispersed. Christ suffered that we should live forever.

For else why should Christ have died? Had He committed anything worthy of death? Why did He clothe Himself in flesh who was invested with glory? And since He was God, why did He become man? And since He reigned in heaven, why did He come down to earth, and become incarnate in the virgin's womb? What necessity, I ask, impelled God to come down to earth, to assume flesh, to be wrapped in swaddling clothes in a manger-cradle, to be nourished with the milk from the breast, to receive baptism from a servant, to be lifted up upon the cross, to be interred in an earthly sepulchre, to rise again the third day from the dead? What necessity, I say, impelled Him to this? It is sufficiently discovered that He suffered shame for man's sake, to set him free from death; and that He exclaimed, as in the words of the prophet, I have endured as a travailing woman. Isaiah 42:14 In very deed did He endure for our sakes sorrow, ignominy, torment, even death itself, and burial. For thus He says Himself by the prophet: I went down into the deep. Jonah 2:4 Who made Him thus to go down? The impious people. Behold, you sons of men, behold what recompense Israel made unto Him! She slew her Benefactor, returning evil for good, affliction for joy, death for life. They slew by nailing to the tree Him who had brought to life their dead, had healed their maimed, had made their lepers clean, had given light to their blind. Behold, you sons of men! Behold, all you people, these new wonders! They suspended Him on the tree, who stretches out the earth; they transfixed Him with nails who laid firm the foundation of the world; they circumscribed Him who circumscribed the heavens; they bound Him who absolves sinners; they gave Him vinegar to drink who has made them to drink of righteousness; they fed Him with gall who has offered to them the Bread of Life; they caused corruption to come upon His hands, and feet who healed their hands and feet; they violently closed His eyes who restored sight to them; they gave Him over to the tomb, who raised their dead to life both in the time before His Passion and also while He was hanging on the tree.

6. For when our Lord was suffering upon the cross, the tombs were burst open, the infernal region was disclosed, the souls leapt forth, the dead returned to life, and many of them were seen in Jerusalem, while the mystery of the cross was being perfected; what time our Lord trampled upon death, dissolved the enmity, bound the strong man, and raised the trophy of the cross, His body being lifted up upon it, that the body might appear on high, and death to be depressed under the foot of flesh. Then the heavenly powers wondered, the angels were astonished, the elements trembled, every creature was shaken while they looked on this new mystery, and the terrific spectacle which was being enacted in the universe. Yet the entire people, as unconscious of the mystery, exulted over Christ in derision; although the earth was rocking, the mountains, the valleys, and the sea were shaken, and every creature of God was smitten with confusion. The lights of heaven were afraid, the sun fled away, the moon disappeared, the stars withdrew their shining, the day came to end; the angel in astonishment departed from the temple after the rending of the veil, and darkness covered the earth on which its Lord had closed His eyes. Meanwhile hell was with light resplendent, for there had the star descended. The Lord, indeed, did not descend into hell in His body but in His Spirit. He forsooth is working everywhere, for while He raised the dead by His body, by His spirit was He liberating their souls. For when the body of the Lord was hung upon the cross, the tombs, as we have said, were opened; hell was unbarred. the dead received their life, the souls were sent back again into the world, and that because the Lord had conquered hell, had trodden down death, had covered the enemy with shame; therefore was it that the souls came forth from Hades, and the dead appeared upon the earth.

7. You see, therefore, how great was the effect of the death of Christ, for no creature endured His fall with equal mind, nor did the elements His Passion, neither did the earth retain His body, nor hell His Spirit. All things were in the Passion of Christ disturbed and convulsed. The Lord exclaimed, as once before to Lazarus, Come forth, you dead, from your tombs and your secret places; for I, the Christ, give unto you resurrection. For then the earth could not long hold the body of our Lord that in it was buried; but it exclaimed, O my Lord, pardon mine iniquities, save me from Your wrath, absolve me from the curse, for I have received the blood of the righteous, and yet I have not covered the bodies of men or Your own body! What is at length this wonderful mystery? Why, O Lord, did You come down to earth, unless it was for man's sake, who has been scattered everywhere: for in every place has Your, fair image been disseminated? Nay! But if you should give but one little word, at the instant all bodies would stand before You. Now, since You have

come to earth, and have sought for the members of Your fashioning, undertake for man who is Your own, receive that which is committed to You, recover Your image, Your Adam. Then the Lord, the third day after His death, rose again, thus bringing man to a knowledge of the Trinity. Then all the nations of the human race were saved by Christ. One submitted to the judgment, and many thousands were absolved. Moreover, He being made like to man whom He had saved, ascended to the height of heaven, to offer before His Father, not gold or silver, or precious stones, but the man whom He had formed after His own image and similitude; and the Father, raising Him to His right hand, has seated Him upon a throne on high, and has made Him to be judge of the peoples, the leader of the angelic host, the charioteer of the cherubim, the Son of the true Jerusalem, the Virgin's spouse, and King for ever and ever. Amen.

6. The Addition in the Codex, with a Various Reading

God, therefore, wishing to visit His own form which He had fashioned after His own image and similitude, has in these last times sent into the world His incorporeal and only Son, who being in the Virgin's womb incarnate, was born perfect man to raise erect lost man, re-collecting His scattered members. For why else should Christ have died? Was He capitally accused? And since He was God, why was He made man? Why did He who was reigning in heaven come down to earth? Who compelled God to come down to earth, to take flesh of the Holy Virgin, to be wrapped in swaddling clothes and laid in a manger, to be nourished with milk, to be baptized in the Jordan, to be mocked of the people, to be nailed to the tree, to be buried in the bosom of the earth, and the third day to rise again from the dead; in the cause of redemption to give life for life, blood for blood, to undergo death for death? For Christ, by dying, has discharged the debt of death to which man was obnoxious. Oh, the new and ineffable mystery! The Judge was judged. He who absolves from sin was bound; He was mocked who once framed the world; He was stretched upon the cross who stretched out the heavens; He was fed with gall who gave the manna to be bread; He died who gives life. He was given up to the tomb who raises the dead. The powers were astonished, the angels wondered, the elements trembled, the whole created universe was shaken, the earth quaked, and its foundations rocked; the sun fled away, the elements were subverted, the light of day receded; because they could not bear to look upon their crucified Lord. The creature, in amazement, said, What is this novel mystery? The judge is judged and is silent; the invisible is seen and is not confounded; the incomprehensible is grasped and is not indignant at it; the immeasurable is contained in a measure and makes no opposition; the impassable suffers and does not avenge its own injury; the immortal dies and complains not; the celestial is buried and bears it with an equal mind. What, I say, is this mystery? The creature surely is transfixed with amazement. But when our Lord rose from death and trampled it down, when He bound the strong man and set man free, then every creature wondered at the Judge who for Adam's sake was judged, at the invisible being seen, at the impassable suffering, at the immortal dead, at the celestial buried in the earth. For our Lord was made man; He was condemned that He might impart compassion; He was bound that He might set free; He was apprehended that He might liberate; He suffered that He might heal our sufferings; He died to restore life to us; He was buried to raise us up. For when our Lord suffered, His humanity suffered, that which He had like man; and He dissolves the sufferings of him who is His like, and by dying He has destroyed death. It was for this cause that He came down upon earth, that by pursuing death He might kill the rebel that slew men. For one underwent the judgment, and myriads were set free; one was buried, and myriads rose again. He is the Mediator between God and man; He is the resurrection and the salvation of all; He is the Guide of the erring, the Shepherd of men who have been set free, the life of the dead, the charioteer of the cherubim, the standard-bearer of the angels, and the King of kings, to whom be glory for ever and ever. Amen.

Milton Keynes UK
Ingram Content Group UK Ltd.
UKHW051105090823
426520UK00023B/662

9 781088 186169